COLOR
your home

CAROL BASS COLOR your home

PHOTOGRAPHY BY DENNIS WELSH

Gibbs Smith, Publisher
Salt Lake City

My appreciation to friends Suzanne Gerry, Patricia O'Shaughnessy, Kathleen Perry, Edgar Allen Beem, Laurie Parlee Hadlock, Sarah Gatchell, Ann Kistler, Liz Poole, and the Maine Cottage crew for contributing to this color book.

First Edition

09 08 07 06 05   10 9 8 7 6 5 4 3 2 1

Text © 2005 Carol Bass
Photographs © 2005 Dennis Welsh

Published by
Gibbs Smith, Publisher
P.O. Box 667
Layton, UT 84041

Orders: 1.800.748.5439
www.gibbs-smith.com

Designed by Pamela Beverly-Quigley, Salt Lake City, Utah
Printed and bound in Hong Kong

Library of Congress Cataloging-in-Publication Data

Bass, Carol.
  Color your home / Carol Bass.—1st ed.
      p. cm.
   ISBN 1-58685-371-6
   1. Color in interior decoration. 2. Color—Psychological aspects. I. Title.
NK2115.5.C6B38 2005
747'.94—dc22
                                    2004024262

Color your home

Introduction

Your Home as Your Canvas

Most people never consider color as a way to change their lives, but it is a simple tool that adds magic to each day. Colors push and pull at our emotions, calling us to embrace life in the boldest of ways. Color adds dashes of madness to a shy life, infuses sensuality into a prim life, and injects raw emotion into our homes. Captivating, inviting rooms make living worthwhile.

Distrustful of our innate creativity, we are often afraid to add color to our homes. Indeed, we are so overscheduled and consumed by work that it is no surprise when we fail to recognize the importance of nurturing our visual senses. We seldom consider the creative part of making our most intimate surroundings—our home—beautiful by way of our own hearts. Yet using color to reawaken our homes is thrilling and soulful work.

How to Use This Book

The first three chapters explore the primary colors: blue, yellow, and red. They possess the purest intensity of all the colors. They sing out wildly and radiate exuberance. The chapters also explore the primary colors' neighboring shades: next door to red are salmon and magenta; next door to blue are aquamarine and lavender; next door to yellow are carrot and maize. Flip through the pages of this book to see beautiful and effective ways for using bold tones. Using these vibrant, rich colors requires you to take a risk, but risk leads to sweet reward.

The final chapter on rustic colors meanders through farm pastures, marsh grasses, and greenhouses. It explores soft, earthy green and garden rose tones that feel comfortable with worn whites and neutrals. Every subtle rustic tone has its own power to heal and energize.

Each chapter centers around three emotions that are evoked by the featured color. Specific ideas for how to incorporate the emotions into your home through the use of color are explained as well as shown. At the end of each chapter, a paint color palette is provided for your reference. Each of the color boxes displays a Benjamin Moore shade (along with the corresponding paint number) that evokes one of the emotions discussed in the chapter. Accent colors that work successfully with each of the shades are provided on the adjacent page.

Benjamin Moore paints are readily available at all major home improvement stores throughout the United States and Canada. You can ask for your favorite Benjamin Moore color by number. Or you can have the store scan the color swatch from this book, and then tell you what the closest paint match would be.

Nature as Your Guide

Nature is the best place to learn about color, for nature is never shy or restrained. Hold a tomato in your hand. Really soak down into those orange-yellow-red tones. Take a daylily petal or a slice of beet and place it on a white piece of paper to purely experience nature's dramatic colors. Hold mussel shells from the beach in your hands. Rub your fingers over their lavender-black tones.

Nature photos throughout this book reveal how colors from the environment provided ideas for the dominant tone in room compositions. Ideas come from ocean water, seaweed, tulips, and sunflowers—from all things of spirit that massage the soul.

When you listen to your heart, your creativity flows. Nurture your own direct emotional connection with color. The process is wild, adventurous, and uncomplicated! Simply step outside into nature; she has all the gifts waiting for you.

Color Balance

The combinations of colors within our homes depend on balance and equilibrium. When a room's composition is creatively balanced and tuned, you feel happy, safe, and full of wonder. A mix of colors should dance and sparkle together, not only in one room but throughout the house.

A colorful composition has three parts: the dominant shades, secondary colors, and spicy accent colors. Think of cooking a savory fish soup. The stock makes up the dominant tones; the vegetables and fish are the secondary shades; and the zesty spices, tossed in at the last minute, make up the accent colors. Why not use rich tones as ingredients in your recipes to spice up your home? The first step is to think in terms of solid color forms. Once you have the composition balanced, then you can introduce minimal touches like striped or floral pillows. Your composition thrives on dialogue with other colors around your home. Provide opportunity for color to be social and sing out from space to space.

In the room settings throughout this book, I've borrowed colors from nature, and then translated these colors into forms that I've moved around like colored pieces of paper in a collage until they make sense. Indeed, colors are like ingredients in a favorite recipe—a dash of magenta, a shake of yellow, a few sprinkles of chive green to perk up the flavor.

Above all, it's important to be adventurous with color. If you think you're not a red person, that red is too emotional or too dynamic, you might be surprised. If you've always felt safe and peaceful with blue, test a lovely green. Zesty orange may seem too powerful, but what punch orange possesses. Take a giant step outside, put your face in a tiger lily, wrap yourself in a field of poppies, and bring those feelings home.

Don't worry about doing something wrong. There are times things will be messy. The only path to success is experience, and experience is composed of a great deal of patience and practice. Remember, white paint erases just about every faux pas. And as Kandinsky said so well, "It must be remembered that an unsuitable combination of form and colour is not necessarily discordant, but may, with manipulation, show the way to fresh possibilities of harmony."

—Carol Bass

COLOR

your home yellow

yellows

Glowing hues of a harvest moon, goldenrod, ripe lemons, and fields of sunflowers.

When Vincent van Gogh and fellow artist Paul Gauguin rented a yellow house and studio in southern France during the late 1800s, Van Gogh was invigorated by the colors around him. The painted yellow structures and golden flowers cast against intense blue skies under a penetrating and brilliant sun made his heart sing. Pairings of complementary colors—rich oranges and cerulean blues, bold reds and lush greens—thrilled him most of all.

Yellows gently and immediately lift our spirits. Those same yellows that inspired Van Gogh can similarly evoke powerful emotional responses when incorporated in our homes. Consider the joys of discovering a sunny yellow house. The owners enjoy life and take pleasure in sharing their cheerfulness with passersby. Bold, luscious blue hydrangeas, red rockers, even the blue sky reflected in the windows are all colors and forms that contribute to this rousing composition. With its bright white trim, the porch is always inviting.

Oh yes! He loved yellow,
did good Vincent . . .
when the two of us were
together in Arles, both of us
insane, and constantly at
war over beautiful colors.
—Paul Gauguin

surprise

Remember when you were a child and discovered your first bird's nest deep in a tangled mass of branches? Yellows have the same power to bring us wonder and surprise each time we walk into a sunny yellow space. Walls washed in sunflower hues inspire creativity and possibility. A maize-toned slipcover or even a small vase of flowers uplifts the spirit. Grass green wicker chairs with striped fabric, red-toned textiles, and a tiny red-striped cabinet add punchy color and pattern. Bright white trim and stone gray cement floors show off all the simple colors and forms.

Color a wall a hushed shade of yellow

Successful use of color requires clutter-free spaces and simple forms. Yellow walls in airy kitchens and small dining spaces are gestures that quietly dazzle family and friends. Yellow entranceways refresh and enliven spirits. These social spaces are perfect for bolder golden hues. Consider applying two glazing layers of paint for greater depth of feeling. Accent touches of marsh grass greens or pomegranate reds from nature complete the composition.

[15]

Yellow hues from outside create charm inside.

optimism

Of all the colors, yellows reflect the greatest amount of sunlight. The sun's rays strike a luminous yellow hue and naturally reflect it back into our minds, steering us toward lively and upbeat conversation. Yellows, radiant and optimistic, are ideal for larger dining areas where conversation around the table is more settled and less salutatory. Libraries and home offices where people work alone and large living areas where friends and family gather to share ideas are all perfect spaces for the more mellow hues of yarrow, pumpkin, and maize.

Infuse a space with hearty yellow accent pieces

A single vase of Shasta daisies offers effortless color possibilities. Small flea market tables or wicker items painted in golden hues are excellent accent pieces that brighten a living area. Flower-stem green mixed with honey wood tones and white trim complete a composition of simple color and form.

[21]

Gardens offer inspiring color combinations in a tucked-away bedroom.

delight

Like the taste of homemade apple pie or
the sound of fine bluegrass music through
an open window, the right shade of
yellow in the right place in your home
can make your soul sing with delight.
Soft, simple bedding and quilts
complement the rich yellow-painted
wooden bed. Mellow goldenrod tones
next to natural wood comfort the mind
and body like fresh air.

Use the hues from a single flower to create a successful color composition in your home

Consider magical color mixtures of a single flower. Study the yellow petals against the deep orange centers and the earthy green stems. These tones make successful choices for slipcovers, kitchen chairs, or painted floors. Use fresh white paint with these shades to brighten your space. The color white is equal to fresh wind. When you use whites with nature's colors, a life-giving space is created.

1
accent
2069-40

2
accent
2001-30

3
accent
2029-40

Choosing Your Yellow*

Surprise
1. 2022-20
2. 2021-30
3. 2022-40

Surprise yellows are wondrous on kitchen and small dining-area walls. To add a splash of unexpected color, paint your kitchen chairs a shade of yellow. Or create your own three tiny yellow paintings using dried yellow flowers from your garden.

Delight
1. 2023-20
2. 2023-40
3. 2023-50

The deep yellow ochre of a daisy's center for dining spaces and light-filled entryways continually delights family and guests. Lighter maize hues bring sunshine to upstairs hallways. A golden yellow–painted front door brightens the day of anyone who passes by.

Optimism
1. 2020-40
2. 2016-30
3. 301

Optimism is created with a steady glow of mellow shades. Old wooden kitchen floors, walls in larger dining areas, and larger living spaces offer ideal surfaces for these wiser yellow tones. Wash dining area walls with two layers of transparent mango or deep carrot.

Accent Colors
1. 2069-40
2. 2001-30
3. 2029-40

Choose fresh yellow apples from the neighborhood market and place them in a blue or green bowl. Toss one ripe red cherry in with the yellow apples and admire the beautiful color combination. Exuberance and energy radiate when colors are allowed to play together.

[28]

*All swatch numbers correspond to Benjamin Moore paint numbers.

1
surprise
2022-20

2
surprise
2021-30

3
surprise
2022-40

1
delight
2023-20

2
delight
2023-40

3
delight
2023-50

1
optimism
2020-40

2
optimism
2016-30

3
optimism
301

COLOR
your home blue

blues

Tranquil hues that flow from the deep purple and aquamarines of deep ocean waters to the ceruleans and lavender of the endless sky.

Artists Marc Chagall and Richard Diebenkorn used blues to create powerful and enchanting paintings. Chagall's *View on the Garden* and *The Painter and His Bride* are both drenched in varying shades of blues that express his deepest emotions. Diebenkorn's abstract landscapes, including *Ocean Park No. 79*, are composed of huge forms with layer upon layer of blues. Like poetry and music, these paintings explore landscape and memory, expressing the intangible through color relationships.

If you are curious and inquisitive, you can create your own poetic spaces in your home through the same process these famous artists painted their canvases. All you need is a little courage, some nerve, and a love of experimentation. Enchanted with the spectrum of emotions the color blue evoked, from serenity and safeness to devotion, Chagall and Diebenkorn continually experimented with a range of blue shades in various pieces of art.

Indigo, cobalt, cerulean, turquoise, violet, and lavender tones soothe our souls and restore us like fresh wind on a summer day. Walls washed with transparent blue layers create a mesmerizing calm in our homes just like the sight of blue wildflowers near alpine streams. Added to colors of sea and sky are shades of lilacs and blueberries, lupines and cornflowers, delphiniums and wild chicory.

[33]

Blue color is everlastingly appointed by the Deity to be a source of delight.
—John Ruskin

serenity

We are healed and nourished by the rhythmic rolling of the sea. The colors created by the sun striking the water restore our spirit and cleanse our jumbled minds. Stress, pressure, and anxiety vanish into the sound of lapping waves. Study the calming interplay of aqua and blue tones as an aquamarine boat skims atop blue water under a bright sky. Blues from nature have that same power to communicate serenity and calm in our interior spaces.

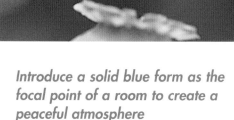

Introduce a solid blue form as the focal point of a room to create a peaceful atmosphere

Bring home the early morning sky blue or the blue-green water of the mountain lake. These tones are comforting choices for slipcovers. They inspire quiet conversation and set the tone for peaceful moments that are ideal for reading or writing.

Don't be afraid to experiment. Wash a wall with pale aqua and then paint large soft-green leaves on top of the aqua, like the Bloomsbury artists of the early 1900s did. If you have a small white room, wash it in pale yellow and paint blue vertical stripes on the walls. Paint with abandon as would an artist painting freestyle pottery.

Bring in colors from the garden to accentuate the water and sky colors. Muted greens of poppy pods and the subtle shades of lilacs and hydrangeas make lovely secondary tones next to the dominant soft blue hues. Add fanciful punches in the form of deep violet and rose throw pillows. Small doses of lime green and cobalt pottery also add brushstrokes of vivid color to the softer dominant blue composition.

Add summer colors to a creamy white space. In a room filled with blue upholstery and trim, experiment with accent dashes of yellow, green, and lavender to inject pep and vitality.

calmness

There is no activity more nourishing than gathering with close friends or family on a porch, wasting time and telling stories. Cedar shingles stained the color of ocean water and porch chairs painted in deep lilac tones make the activity even more glorious.

Blues from nature used in interior spaces generate emotions of calmness, trust, and security. People feel safe and protected when they are surrounded by blue, and this feeling of calmness awakens in them hope and confidence, humor and comfort. An old flea market table painted blue has the charm of a favorite old sweater or a pair of boots that you never throw away. A home that uses blue is calm, sound, and thoughtful.

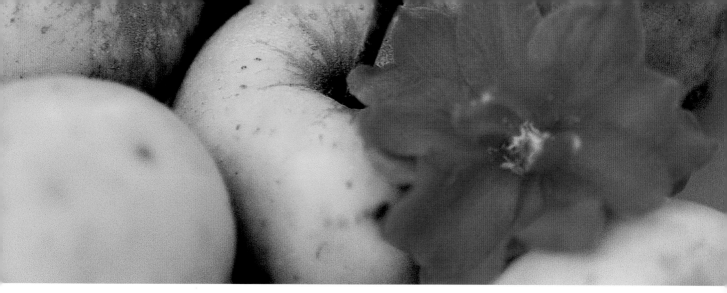

Blue and white creates charm

Blue and white is a highly appealing color combination, which evokes the sense of calmness you feel when you're sailing on a clear summer day. A mix of bright white walls and blue upholstery welcomes the spice of accent colors to add mystery and fun. Pep up blue and white with bold yellow and lipstick pink throw pillows. Bright ceramics in lime, olive, rose, and yellow add joy. An old, green metal stool and a flea market table add charm and soften the newer pieces. A subtle white-painted floor shows off all the boldly colored forms in the room.

A lively blue and white bunkroom expresses an atmosphere of joy and security for children.

devotion

All who sit and sip coffee or tea in this sunny yellow room with blue-painted rattan furniture, green plants, and bowl of rosy red pears feel a sense of warm devotion. Clutter-free rooms composed of simple forms and pure color, with bright white accents, are fresh and airy. Colorful fruits and flowers provide ideas for accent colors. A blush-colored throw or an area rug with bold rose and mossy green forms would work well in this airy space.

***Even a tiny space can be
welcoming and radiant***

A charming hallway with an old
painted wooden floor is warm and
cheery. Guests feel like family, and
family members feel at home in this
space. Details, like the accent colors
from a green slicker and red dog dish,
enliven the entire space and create a
comfortable, adventurous, and loving
ambiance. A sky blue–painted floor
immediately eases and relaxes guests.

Choosing Your Blue*

Serenity
1. 2066-50
2. 2056-50
3. 2037-40

Soft, serene blues are ideal for bedrooms, baths, and dining areas. In a child's bedroom or small guest room, paint large floral green designs on top of soft blue hues. Be sure to sketch the forms with a pencil first. Consider green-blues for airy dining spaces and soft sky blues on old wooden floors.

Calmness
1. 2069-40
2. 2067-40
3. 2067-20

Intense ocean blue linen for slipcovers is bold and bright and inspires thoughts of calm, safe harbors. Paint daring large aqua and white diagonal squares on kitchen and dining room floors. Paint a tucked-away bath a barely there aqua tint, keeping trim white. Introduce accent shades by hanging colored towels.

Devotion
1. 2056-70
2. 2066-40
3. 2056-40

A front door painted a lapis or indigo hue shows love, devotion, and careful thought. Violets and cobalt blues are appealing accent shades for bedroom area rugs and quilts. Place deep blue antique pottery vases filled with fresh flowers in kitchens and bedrooms.

Accent Colors
1. 174
2. 1313
3. 573

Create your own paintings of bananas in red bowls or giant red pears on yellow backgrounds to hang in a room with blue walls. Choose toss pillows that have red, ochre, and citrus green tones to snap up your blues.

*All swatch numbers correspond to Benjamin Moore paint numbers.

1
serenity
2066-50

2
serenity
2056-50

3
serenity
2037-40

1
calmness
2069-40

2
calmness
2067-40

3
calmness
2067-20

2
devotion
2066-40

3
devotion
2056-40

COLOR
your home red

reds

*Life-giving hues of
the heart, crackling
fires, summer
raspberries, and
sunset skies.*

Henri Matisse painted his famous *Harmony in Red* in 1908. His composition is drenched in bold, rich reds. Just as the dominant red tone in his painting succeeds because of the colors around it, so, too, do the red tones in your home. Red tones enjoy dialogue with other reds throughout in your home.

Reds have vitality and mystery. Reds release unexplored and unexpressed energy. Conversely, reds can convey a slow-burning energy and gentle passion—a passion that speaks of life and breath, and says, "I am exuberant, I am here, and I am alive." While the idea of reds in our home frightens many, the rewards are magnificent.

Introducing red to a lifeless space adds charisma, making us sit up a little straighter. Scarlet hues of sensuous poppies in the grass are visual poetry. Fertile clay reds speak of history and geology and connect us to the earth and its primitive tribes. Red has the visual impact of dancing the tango. Reds bring out deep-down emotions of passion, zest, and power.

passion

Use daubs of red in your home
composition as if you were painting
with a bold brush. Each stroke
expresses your passionate emotions
and innate creativity. Just like the roses
in your garden, reds create moments of
excitement throughout interior spaces.
Experiment with a small touch of red at
first, like a rosy hall table that bounces
to life in front of a white-painted wood
wall. Strokes of blue on the tuft stool
and the golden yellow of the brass add
spoonfuls of spice.

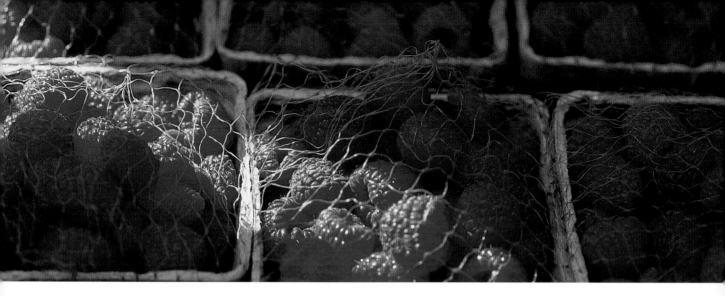

Introduce red into your home to create hearty dialogue with other colors in the whole-house composition

One red patch in an environment rivets the eye, and the heart sings, "I am truly alive at this moment!" Notice the dialogue that occurs among red and the other colors when you pass a red chair on a porch, red blueberry bushes in an autumn field, red peppers at the farmers market, or even a contemporary painting with one red brushstroke in a museum. Red works when it can converse with other tones nearby.

When the front-porch door is opened, the watermelon red deck chair in the photo on the opposite page speaks with rosy swirling forms in a hallway rug and a deeper red rose on painted kitchen chairs.

Earthy orange and deep red walls work because the accent colors—sky blues and spruce greens—give them radiant life. Natural wood floors and white trim soften and brighten the colors. The setting is composed of simple forms, uncluttered space, natural light, and fresh air.

zest

Zest has positive and stimulating energy. All of the colors in this space convey that steady comfort and happiness. Accent colors of maize and egg yolk yellows, mossy greens, slate blues, and salmon and papaya reds punch up the dominant tone of the rosy zinnia sofa. This setting is a successful use of solid rich colors on pure forms that dance on white-painted canvas.

***One rosy chair in a room
adds a zesty ambiance
that sparkles continuously***

Each time you enter a pleasurable
space, you feel a soft, glowing energy.
Zest can come from a single deep-lily-
rose-upholstered chair. Energy and life,
felt in constant heartbeat moments, can
be created with throw pillows in shades
of soft, saturated poppy. Invigorating
atmospheres exude from walls washed
in shades of watermelon and zinnia.

Harmonies created through use of red hues on walls, painted stools, and fabric flourish in a mix of light, space, and bright white trim. Nature's winning hues—banana yellow, leaf green, and rusty pollen—succeed as accent colors.

power

The simpler the red form, the more powerful the energy. The forms and colors of white bags full of crabapples inspire this room's composition. The vitality of a single red maple leaf on black pavement or the glimpse of a bold red cardinal at the feeder connect us to nature instantly. The bold red slipcover on a sofa and the small red table dazzle in this neutral setting as do red dahlias in the garden. Small, spicy brushstrokes of lavender, coral, yellow, and aqua in an area rug's border add energy and life.

Paint a door a brilliant red tone to create a dominant and hearty greeting

Simple red tones in nature hint at ways to use color. A deep velvety red berry shining in the afternoon sun, surrounded by green and umber tones, or a bright red robin in an early-spring landscape remind us of the brilliant power red hues possess. A bold red front door cheers and welcomes us home. A chair, table, or wall painted the color of a pomegranate have the same powerful presence within your home.

1
accent
300

2
accent
817

3
accent
2024-30

Choosing Your Red*

Passion
1. 2079-30
2. 2004-20
3. 2077-10

Earthy red walls create passionate warmth and radiance in living spaces. Natural light, white trim, and the tones of warm wood and stone are inviting and alive. Salmon red walls in kitchens or fire engine red kitchen chairs light small fires of passion.

Zest
1. 2087-20
2. 2001-20
3. 2016-10

Saturated rusty orange slipcovers with deep pink piping are unusual, offering surprising opportunities to incorporate simple, zesty forms of color. Two layers of translucent chili-pepper-colored walls, painted white trim, and an accent punch of a celadon chair and desk enliven the home office. Remember, colors are successful when they have dialogue throughout the home.

*All swatch numbers correspond to Benjamin Moore paint numbers.

Power
1. 2086-30
2. 2000-30
3. 2086-20

Two washed layers of soft poppy red in a living space create a feeling of power and intimacy. A muted Chinese red is unusual and unexpected for a guest bedroom. In a monochromatic space, peony-painted flea market tables give a small, powerful punch.

Accent Colors
1. 300
2. 817
3. 2024-30

Just as chives, dill, and pepper can be added to spice up a soup, using dashes of yellow, lavender, and spring greens enliven your dominant reds and create a winning composition.

[72]

1
passion
2079-30

2
passion
2004-20

3
passion
2077-10

1
zest
2087-20

2
zest
2001-20

3
zest
2016-10

1
power
2086-30

2
power
2000-30

3
power
2086-20

COLOR

your home rustic

rustics
Muted hues that are worn with the patina of seasons and formed over time by nature's sun, wind, and water.

Rustics are down-to-earth colors that radiate the warmness of life. Rustic hues can be found on worn wooden skiffs and bags of boiled peanuts. We can bring home the color of roasting oysters, wild oats on the beach, hay bales, and old tractors to use in our living spaces.

Rustics are mellow colors of textured objects—wooden baskets, shells, leather, stone, rusty metal, and bone—that have their own histories. Their genuine surfaces invite touch and rouse wonder. Cedar shingles have authenticity; plastic shingles don't. Old metal mailboxes have spirit that plastic molded mailboxes will never have.

The ripeness of secondary shades—rose, purple, aqua, salmon, green—work as accent colors to spice up the rustics. The brilliant hues of fruits and flowers complement the delicate rustics. Rustic tones evoke emotions of vitality, wholeness, and contentment.

[77]

Bring home color possibilities from a walk across an open field. The serendipity of one pine tree, the flash of a scarlet tanager, or the drop of one green apple are all gifts of color.
—Carol Bass

vitality

There are rustic moments each day that carry the thread of life's vitality. Walking down the dirt road in front of this house, we feel connected to the people inside. The worn textures and colors are inviting and full of life. The authentic materials, cedar shingles and wood siding, have an energy that touches us as we pass by. The dominant bright whites of the home enlighten and the secondary shades of the gray roof and black trim of the windows anchor that energy. The yellow flowers, the hint of faded coral on the curtains, and the silvery leaf greens spice up the rustic setting with dashes of flavor.

Infuse vitality into rustic white rooms by using soft accent touches

Rustic honey-toned wood floors and white-painted paneling compose a sensuous environment for floral textiles. The uncluttered white space welcomes fresh air and bits of garden color. Consider washing the bedroom walls in the soft salmon-rose hues from the chairs. The walls will look stunning next to natural pine floors, a white bed and white trim, and an old flea market table. Colorful antique quilts and woolen blankets with maize, rose, and moss tones allow the energy of old and new to flow together. Use spots of warm salmon throughout your home's composition. Colors are social like we are; they enjoy camaraderie with other tones around your home.

[81]

Use sky blues and aqua to wash the walls of a rustic bedroom. Bone white furniture gleams with natural pine floors. A simple green chair spices like freshly diced chives.

wholeness

This setting radiates a fresh-air, out-in-the-woods feeling of wholeness that's inviting and cozy. Horizontal textured wallboards finished with a lichen green wash combined with golden wood pine floors unify a background that's comforting and sensual. The moss-painted bed and the white bedding and wicker tables, details of color and form, deepen the composition and connect the interior space to the woods and clouds outside the window. Tiny brushstrokes of black from the framed original paintings and prints, like exclamation marks, add a robust dash to the space.

Add splashes of bold color to rustic rooms to ripen your setting

Simple forms and colors in quiet, uncluttered spaces radiate calm, flowing energy. Paint your walls and floors shell white using accent tones from poppies, daffodils, and cornflowers for punch. Consider upholstery in deep red petal shades against bone white walls. Exclamation points of black add just enough drama.

[87]

Bring home colors of an antique farmhouse dressed in worn gray and bright, unexpected aqua underneath a vivid blue sky. Sensual scarlet gladiolas and soft green leaves add spice and snap to the setting.

contentment

Most of the time, the simplest touches are all that are needed to create a gratifying, nourishing space. Floral antique textiles make lovely curtains in a sun-drenched, white-painted bath. Use colors from gladiola and dahlia petals for slipcovers and pillows. Paint a flea market side table mango or citrus green to add spice. Place a vase of wildflowers on the counter. All colors work together when a space is uncluttered and warm white is used for trim and doors.

By using nature's colors in our homes, exteriors and interiors dance together, making us feel whole and connected to nature

Use outside colors inside. Consider the colors of a velvety chartreuse moss and fern growing over and through silver granite, a dark green canoe stored on sawhorses, and a rusted red wheelbarrow. Bring bark, leaf, and stone colors from woods to porches, and then continue their tones inside. Painted wicker, white-painted paneling, green plants, the warm wood of floors and doors are all authentic materials that create a nourishing space. Use moss green denim, linen slipcovers, or lichen-painted walls touched with accents of tulip pink and rusty orange.

1
accent
2070-40

2
accent
2024-10

3
accent
1314

Choosing Your Rustic*

Vitality
1. 2137-60
2. 2153-50
3. 2167-60

Off-white, sage white, and popcorn-colored walls convey quiet vigor in dining rooms and home offices. Used in bedrooms, these tones shine with the fullness of an autumn pasture. Paint a dining-area floor in wheatgrass and add antique grange chairs painted in spruce green or cranberry red tones for spice.

Wholeness
1. 2151-60
2. 2148-60
3. 2148-50

Sea-biscuit white and moss-striped upholstery surrounded by brown and gray-toned walls and white trim in living spaces offer peace and calm. One poppy- or tomato-painted end table adds spirit. Use a weathered garden bench for a coffee table. Fill an ironstone pitcher with colorful flowers from your garden.

Contentment
1. HC-1
2. 2113-60
3. 2047-60

Sage green, moss green, and teal doors add depth and stillness to muted stone- and sand-colored walls. Combine soft rustic linens and bedding with antique quilts and bark-cloth pillows. Fill your child's pottery bowls with shells or stones you have gathered on your walks.

Accent Colors
1. 2070-40
2. 2024-10
3. 1314

Blue, mustard, and deep red tones work well with muted rustic hues. They add a splash of liveliness and glamour to the understated exquisiteness of quiet rustic hues.

*All swatch numbers correspond to Benjamin Moore paint numbers.

1
vitality
2137-60

2
vitality
2153-50

3
vitality
2167-60

1
wholeness
2151-60

2
wholeness
2148-60

3
wholeness
2148-50

1
contentment
HC-1

2
contentment
2113-60

3
contentment
2047-60

Resources

Benjamin Moore Paints

To learn more about
Benjamin Moore paints
and to locate a store near you, go to
www.benjaminmoore.com

Maine Cottage

888.859.5522
www.mainecottage.com

Carol Bass

Carol Bass Design
314 Littlejohn Island
Yarmouth, ME 04096
207.846.5414
www.carolbasscottage.com